START YOUR OWN SENIOR TRASPORTATION BUSINESS

DISCOVER HOW YOU CAN EARN $35 TO $60 AN HOUR DRIVING SENIORS TO MEDICAL APPOINTMENTS.

MARK SANDERS

TABLE OF CONTENTS

INTRODUCTION

A transportation business is basically any business that has a hand in transporting individuals or goods. It can also have to do with giving transportation to different business owners who need assistance connecting their item to their genuine business.

These days, it is uncommon to go seven days without finding out about the challenges and costs of transportation, especially in metropolitan centers. The biggest trouble for some, seniors is that their needs are unique in relation to those of metropolitan and suburban workers and students, and one system cannot be everything to all individuals.

Seniors are in the minority with regards to transit and street users thus there is a characteristic dread that their voice will be overwhelmed and their needs left neglected as the system focuses on fixing the issue of moving millions of individuals consistently to work and school at basically the same time.

At the point when we analyze the transportation needs of seniors, we have to recognize that we are truly discussing those seniors who are not, at this point ready to drive. Until we reach about age 75, seniors transportation needs are not generally all that vastly different from every other person as driving personal vehicles is the staggering method of transportation. At age 75, notwithstanding, we start to retire from driving at a genuinely consistent and persistent rate and by age 85 we shift from most of individuals heading to most of individuals done driving.

The key is to understand the extra challenges past getting starting with one course then onto the next course that are made when someone gives up driving. This includes perceiving the increased open door for isolation and loneliness that can happen. The main solution for individuals when they retire from driving is to get everything conveyed. We may think we are productively addressing their requirement for groceries and medications that are presently dropped off versus gotten, yet we are also cutting the person off from the everyday social interactions that originate from shopping and visiting the pharmacy. The requirement for someone to go with a slight senior is also a restricting variable keeping numerous seniors housebound and we have to remember it is transporting the senior and their partner, yet in addition ensuring they can discover a friend on the off chance that we are to completely meet the transportation need.

In any case, today, you can discover businesses that take into account well off seniors. In the event that you need your new business to succeed, you should offer an ideal transportation that is required in the territory where you are servicing. The transportation business can be used to take seniors to social gatherings, meetings, and special appointments. There are disabled seniors that you can also focus on yet before you choose this specialty, you should decide whether there are many disabled individuals in your general vicinity. Choosing the correct vehicle is imperative. Vehicle manufacturers are currently creating special transportation for the elderly.

Transportation is urgent to ensure access to essential services such as clinical care and shopping for food. The accessibility of sufficient transportation enables more seasoned persons to live freely in their communities, helps to forestall isolation and the possible requirement for long haul care position. Numerous more seasoned individuals, who do not drive, must depend on loved ones to give a significant part of the transportation. In any case, for others, it is necessary to discover network resources to give transportation, as this imperative support service might be their lone association with the outside world.

Transportation services shift in communities relying on where you live. Types of transportation that might be accessible for the elderly, is singular way to-entryway service, fixed course with scheduled services, or ridesharing with volunteer drivers. A decent spot to start your search for transportation is your neighborhood on Aging. In some communities the Area Agency on Aging orchestrate, screen, and support programs that give transportation to the elderly. Regardless of whether your nearby organization does not give transportation services straightforwardly, they should have the option to give assistance for discovering help.

Regardless of whether you are searching for yourself, a relative or a companion, consider what sort of service would best address your issues. Door - to- door service refers to transportation starting with one specific area then onto the next, requiring notification ahead of time. This kind of service is based upon request and allows the most adaptability. Fixed course and scheduled services transport riders along an established course with foreordained stops at designated locations. In spite of the fact that this service provides less adaptability and fees on a for each ride basis that might be discounted for seniors, early bookings are not needed. Ridesharing programs for the most part organize more seasoned persons requiring rides to be transported to specific destinations such as senior centers, grown-up day care, and health-related appointments with volunteer drivers.

As referenced, fees are usually required for some way to-entryway services and on an expense for every ride for fixed transportation services however regularly with senior discounted rates.

Numerous communities have created volunteer programs with insignificant or no cost with the assistance and support of their neighborhood Aging.

Besides, building a senior transportation business is

much easier than starting most different businesses because it is a service business that does not need a store or stock. The need in our present world is developing fast for senior transport drivers because of the huge number of aging individuals who cannot drive anymore and need a ride to clinical appointments, shopping and social events.

The substantial data is do not believe that since it is easy to start, that it is without rivalry. To be sure, furious competitions exist amongst businesses in this industry. Most individuals in this business are small businesses run by a person with restrictions to a specific neighborhood.

You have to figure out how to persuade individuals to trust you instead of their preferred neighborhood senior driver. Also, for you to stay applicable, you should have the option to convey consistent quality service, be inventive and you should have the option to meet the expectations of individuals and your customers.

SENIOR TRANSPORTATION IN THE PRESENT WORLD

Transportation is one of the top challenges' seniors across the globe stress over. Having the option to get where we should be, the point at which we should be there, proves more troublesome as we age, especially once we are not, at this point ready to drive. While gridlock, long commutes, and rising costs are the significant transportation issues for some, working-aged individuals, most seniors face various issues that require various solutions. Furthermore, the consequences of not meeting the transportation needs of seniors, especially those who cannot drive anymore, can be costly to the citizen. In the event that a senior is not ready to dependably get to clinical appointments or keep up social connections, there is a lot of proof to suggest that their health will be legitimately affected, which can prompt costly services such as visits to the crisis office and situation in long haul care facilities.

There is nobody solution that will satisfy the transportation needs everything being equal. Some solutions have structural limitations while others have financial constraints; in any case, all solutions require governments, and seniors themselves, to perceive the commitment they each must make if improvements are to be possible.

The age of 65 is at present used to characterize a "senior" and it has customarily been the age when one retires from the paid work power. While the capacity to authorize obligatory retirement at age 65 was wiped out in some aspect of the world some years prior, and the extent of seniors working past the age of 65 continues to increase, it is also discovered that even at 65 years old, 72% of seniors are not working, yet around 90% have a driver's license and use personal vehicles as their essential method of transportation. Thus, the vast dominant part of seniors establishes their retirement lifestyle driving themselves to activities and appointments.

In any case, the extent of the populace that holds a functioning driver's license declines with age, and the pace of decay is a lot steeper than the pace of utilitarian decrease. What this means in down to earth terms is, on the off chance that you are 85-year-old you are likely living freely (82%), without dementia (80%) and do not need a wheelchair (96%), however you not, at this point hold a functioning driver's license (56%).

After age 85, the extent of seniors who are not, at this point effectively driving far exceeds the extent of seniors who are living in residential care or assisted living where transportation needs are basically met by office operators and additionally services are conveyed nearby. It is imperative to perceive the developing dynamic of seniors who wish to stay as free as possible and engaged with their communities, friends, and families, yet are not, at this point ready to drive.

The need and desire for seniors to get all over town for appointments and socialization does not drastically decrease as they age. What does decrease is their capacity to drive themselves to where they have to go.

WHY START A SENIOR TRANSPORT BUSINESS?

Mature age no uncertainty is an interesting phase of life. Nonetheless, it also has its own challenges. It is exceptionally obvious that as individuals come to their 60's, various things will in general occur or rather a great deal of things will in general change. A ton of them can never again be working all day jobs, implying that they will spend a ton of time in their homes.

As they stay at home, some will lose their freedom through illness, strokes and vision weakness.

A great deal of the seniors who end up with these issues will either surrender their driver's licenses at the request of a specialist or relative. Despite the fact that we concur this is basically for safety reasons; it essentially leaves the seniors 'caught' in their homes along these lines making a business open door for you.

Note that with numerous seniors who do not have friends or family living close by, moving ceaselessly from home for even a simple task like getting mail at the post office or going to a clinical arrangement becomes a significant stress. Most times, the senior may choose to just stay indoors instead of depending on taxi services which can be a costly outing midtown or to the pharmacy.

One of the businesses that come in truly convenient now in life is a senior transportation business. For sure, a senior transportation service will be a cost-successful option for a great deal of seniors who might need to play out some duties or run barely any chores themselves. Starting your senior transportation service would be faster and easier than most different businesses.

This is because there is no conventional preparing required. All you will require is a dependable vehicle, great and simple hierarchical skills, having the option to speak with seniors with persistence, understanding and compassion and want to offer an assistance that helps your customers as much as it will support you.

Anything concerning the elderly services industry will continue blasting and growing. Helped by an aging populace, the services that can be offered is bountiful.

Then, an important segment of the services gave to this aspect of the populace are finished by institutional providers for example nursing care and assisted-living facilities instead of from the industry's formal, non-institutional providers. In any case, it is accepted that in the coming years, the income lined up with the seniors will develop significantly, basically because of the kept aging of the populace.

The developing significance of transportation services in the healthcare system has designed income development for the transportation Services industry in the course of recent years. Healthcare reforms have permitted more insured individuals to use industry services, in this way boosting income.

Experts accept that in the years to come, the developing number of individuals aged 65 and more established will sustain industry development, since the elderly experience more clinical issues than more youthful groups, and consolidation inside the industry will improve working proficiency and costs.

Without a doubt, according to the name of this business, we do not have to stress our brains to understand those needing this worthwhile business. With 40 million

Americans over the age 65 and 6 million more than 85, the senior services business has become a bungalow industry, requiring everybody from home health care workers to gardeners to fall counteraction specialists.

Individuals inside this age will in general think that it's hard to get standard things done which is the reason by offering a support that gives them the chance to carry on with a free life, you can be rest assured that you are serving God, man and your pocket.

Statistics have it that one in each five seniors more than 65 does not drive, and need to get to and from clinical appointments, such as a visit to their PCP or physical therapist. Also, just like the rest of us, non-driving seniors need to go out to shop, gotten things done, visit friends and go to social events. The fast-developing interest for private senior transportation services has made a tremendous open door for those who can give rides to seniors and others who cannot drive.

CHAPTER - 1

UNDERSTANDING YOUR SENIOR CUSTOMERS

On the off chance that you or your adored one is not, at this point ready to drive, there are personal transportation options through states programs, non-profits and private businesses. A case of an extraordinary alternative for senior transportation is Gogograndparent. They offer a helpful and moderate solution for seniors to get around. The safe transportation of seniors is significant, which is the reason Gogograndparent is one of the most loved services most especially in America.

Did you realize that one-portion of Americans 65 and more seasoned do not approach public transportation? Furthermore, that the greater part of all non-drivers 65 and more established stay at home in a given day because they do not have transportation options. Those in country areas and small towns are especially influenced because the transportation options are restricted.

In any case, it is significant for seniors to stay portable to keep their social freedom with friends and family;

to diminish feelings of isolation and loneliness, and numerous other life-dragging out benefits.

Seniors keep driving "as long as possible because they are uninformed of, or do not accept they have, elective means of transportation."

Seniors "limit their driving or stop driving inside and out because of practical difficulties."

"When they stop driving, numerous more seasoned adults are so disabled that they cannot use most open and para-transit systems."

•   **Clinical Transportation Options**

Discovering transportation to go to the supermarket, or to visit friends, is a certain something. Discovering transportation to go to a regular checkup is another issue completely. Showing up to these appointments, regardless of whether it be a test, a clinical technique, or just a customary test, is indispensable to your health.

Because of this, depending on open transportation probably will not be the best alternative in clinical situations. Luckily, when clinical necessity is a factor, certain different options are made less expensive and more helpful.

•   **Insurance Covered Transportation**

Contingent upon your insurance supplier, your health inclusion may incorporate a specific measure of transportation for clinical purposes. In that case, a vehicle, van, or other vehicle will get you at your home and take you to your arrangement. There may, nonetheless, be limitations, such as the quantity of trips you can take every month. Call your insurance supplier and discover what your options are and how to exploit them.

In the event that you have Medicaid, a significant measure of your clinical transportation is secured. On the off chance that you have Medicare, notwithstanding, at that point shockingly, transportation to schedule specialist's visits probably will not be accessible to you through your insurance. In any case, contingent upon your situation, you might have the option to use a rescue vehicle in certain non-crisis situations, in the event that you have a composed note from your doctor, stating that different forms of transportation are a risk to your health, and an emergency vehicle is medicinally necessary.

- **Ease Alternatives**

Regardless of whether your insurance does not cover transportation to schedule medical checkups, there are frequently autonomous services you can investigate. Numerous areas have neighborhood organizations that give minimal effort, non-crisis clinical transportation to seniors who do not drive, and additionally have restricted portability. Once more, do your research and discover what services are advantageous to you, and what their options are.

- **Paying for Transportation**

Regardless of whether it is significant clinical transportation or just a common outing into town, when you have secured your ride, you have to know how you are paying for it. On the off chance that you are living on a fixed salary, this probably won't be easy to do. Public transit may just be a couple of dollars, however when you are on a limited spending plan, each dollar counts. So, what would you be able to do to cover, or if nothing else relieve, the costs of transportation?

- **Senior Discounts**

On the off chance that you use public transit, numerous cities offer senior discounts, in some structure. You may need to register for a specific program, or apply for a special senior bus or train pass, or make some other move so as to exploit the diminished toll. Some cities even permit seniors to ride public transportation complimentary! Research your territory's various forms of public transportation and see what they offer.

As referenced before, numerous communities also have special, regularly non-benefit and volunteer-based services, which give clinical and different forms of transportation to seniors who need assistance getting around. These services are regularly entryway to entryway, and might be offered easily or even complimentary.

- ### **Assisted Living Services**

On the off chance that you are living in an assisted living community, at that point the office itself may offer its own transportation services, or collaborate with a free service. They may furnish you with a discounted rate, or the cost up to a specific sum might be remembered for your month to month lease. Ask what options they have accessible. Regardless of whether they do not have their own minimal effort transportation options, they can likely suggest some in the territory that can address your issues and your spending plan.

- ### **Significant Distance Transportation**

You have transportation around your locale secured, yet consider the possibility that you have to go across the nation. Perhaps you are moving to another state. Perhaps an old companion has had a crisis, and you have to go to them. Possibly you just need to take some time off. Whatever the circumstances, travel can be hard as you get more established. However, that does not mean it is impossible. So, it is essential to realize how to deal with it, if and when the situation arises.

- ### **Starting Considerations**

The first interesting point is your general health. Certain conditions can make travel troublesome or awkward, including; Physical Disabilities, Arthritis, Heart Disease, Diabetes, Colostomy, Sickle Cell Disease and Mental Health Issues.

Converse with your doctor before you leave, to see if

any clinical issues may make a significant distance trip troublesome, or on the off chance that they have any recommendations for how to travel, or what should be possible to make it easier.

You also need to decide how you will travel. Will someone be driving you? Will you be flying? Will you be taking a train or a bus? Furthermore, will you travel alone, or will someone else go with you?

Especially on the off chance that you have restricted versatility, it is smarter to go with a close companion or relative. Someone who knows your clinical history and knows about your needs can support you if any issues arise, and give appropriate data in case of a crisis.

At long last, the national government requires each state to give transportation to and from clinical appointments for each patient on Medicaid. Most states use autonomous brokers to schedule rides for patients, so simply registering with your state's merchant can give lots of steady work.

CHAPTER - 2

BUSINESS START UP BASIC

Starting any business is troublesome. It takes difficult work and commitment. Starting a senior transportation organization is the same. You should research other senior transportation businesses in your general vicinity and decide the market for the service. You will also need to do an industry analysis for the business plan. Use the industry analysis to educate your estimates for the financial model, which will incorporate estimates for complete revenues and absolute expenses. Start small, using one vehicle first, and afterward develop your activity as your interest grows.

So, you have chosen to start a senior transportation business. It is a good thought and sure it will do well simply because the odds are in support of yourself.

At last, the quantity of seniors in our communities is enormous and increasing consistently and at a fast movement. This ensures there will be likely customers to draw from for some, numerous years to come. That is the reason you should be sure this is the business you need to dispatch. When you have discovered that, you also need to know a couple of extra things. This section of the book will make a short list of key items to consider when starting up a senior transportation business.

These key items may not seem too hard to follow, yet are essential in the beginning phases of building up your senior transportation business plan.

Well before you toss make the ways for what will most surely turn into a beneficial senior transportation business, you have to do a couple of things first. The accompanying list of key elements you have to have set up before you start booking clients will ensure your success.

1. Legal Structure

This step will set your business separated from any competitors as it will unmistakably characterize the establishment of your business. You should choose early in the event that you will work your senior transportation service as a sole proprietorship or as a Limited Liability Company. Each has advantages and disadvantages. Each will have diverse assessment implications and each will have an alternate bearing on how you will have the option to grow your business with the expansion of more employees or vehicles.

2. Licensing

The legitimate option to work your business will originate from various levels of licensing. This will incorporate a business license for the network you plan to offer your types of assistance. You may also require state so it is wise to sort those details out ahead of schedule.

3. Business Name

The character you make with your business name is urgent. It will be the means by which customers will distinguish you and you will need it to extend a decent, positive picture. In light of this, your business name should be easy to recall, say something about the sort of business it is and sound professional and mindful.

4. Supplies

You will require some extra things to keep your senior transportation service working smoothly. This will incorporate office supplies and some other thing you will require at work. It might mean a wireless, arrangement calendars, charging programs on a PC alongside the PC.

On the off chance that you are starting small with non-Medicaid customers, a smart telephone with the privilege apps can deal with your appointments and scheduling. Be that as it may, for enormous scale, you will require something other than a phone and a vehicle. You should deal with your business appropriately and expertly; you have to realize how to connect and deal with issues when the need arises. Extra things you will need may incorporate;

- Vehicles

- Drivers

- Garages

- Dispatch systems

- Top lights

- Taxi meters

- GPS

- Electronic transaction systems

- Taxi driver security screens

- Safety cameras for taxis

- Decals, labels and uniform

5. Service Schedule

What kinds of deliveries do you see yourself doing so as to make a gainful senior transportation business? Obviously, you will wind up building your service around pickups and drop offs. Some clients may require a ride to appointments and you may also wind up heading out to get groceries notwithstanding the ordinary chores you plan to offer. The service schedule is practically the 'menu' of what you can offer. Consider it carefully as you may see additional opportunities originating from past your basic get or drop off arrangement.

6. Pricing

This is the thing that will have the effect between your business being beneficial and not, the value you charge your customers. Your area will have some impact on valuing with cities gaining closer to the head of the scale with rustic communities procuring closer to the low finish of the scale. Plus, it is wise to see what services you intend to offer that can be consolidated and charged out at a slightly lower rate.

7. Promotion

The best method to get customers is to advertise your business. While there is a cost appended to most forms of advertising, there are ways to advance your business that will cost you close to nothing over the long haul. Business cards, posters, vehicle signage and systems administration for contacts will all serve to channel traffic to your business.

In the event that you are thinking about how to start a transportation business, first consider the entirety of the possibilities. This book to starting a transportation business can enable you to characterize what a transportation business is and will go over all that you have to start your very own transportation business. It takes a great deal of arranging, yet you can successfully start a business in the event that you are prepared to commit time to it.

When you complete these key items, you will be that a lot closer to having a beneficial senior transportation business. Inability to finish these items will hugely affect your success.

Possible shortcomings of Starting a Senior

Transportation Business

Undoubtedly, the senior transportation industry has encountered and will keep appreciating development trends to a great extent because of the rising care and clinical needs of seniors, and lawful decisions that empower disabled individuals have equivalent access to social activities.

By and large, most companies close to or in the industry will in general specialize in clinical transportation; while others transport disabled and elderly individuals to and from day-care programs, social events and different activities. Possible threats to this business may incorporate;

- Market research and feasibility

- Penetrating the market

- Employing experienced workers

- Gaining tolerance in dealing with your clients and so on.

HOW TO CHOOSE A GOOD BUSINESS NAME FOR YOUR SENIOR TRANSPORTATION BUSINESS?

As troublesome as it might be to think, concocting the ideal business name is not an easy task. In any event, for a senior transportation business. At the point when you need to consider the drawn-out effects of a business name, it will be joined to you and your business everlastingly and you will need one that works and keeps laboring for several years. This section will serve as a guide for you in choosing the best name possible for your business with these accommodating tips.

- **Keep It Easy**

While choosing a business name, you have to recall it has to be an easy one. At the end of the day, it needs to be easy to articulate, spell and recollect. Plus, on the off chance that it will be essential for a website space name it has to be easy to not be confused with sound the same words. For instance, if your website is JanesSeniorService.com you might need to transform it to forestall misspellings like JanesSeniorsService.com.

- **Avoid Trendy or Cute**

Trends do not last until the end of time. This is the reason you have to choose a business name that is timeless and does not sound obsolete over some undefined time frame. Jane's Disco Seniors Service sounds retro yet likely not as professional as Jane's Seniors Service does. The same goes for adorable spellings as Janez Seniors Service will be difficult to find on the web and is as acceptable as invisible if customers cannot discover you. The plan to remember is that your customers are seniors. They have to recollect a name that is easy yet not the same as the various business names secured away their memory. You do not need your business name to mix into others as that will make it difficult to recollect as well. When you pick a name, ask seniors on the off chance that it would be one they could recollect whether they needed to.

FOCUS ON THE BUSINESS PURPOSE

While choosing your business name, attempt to cause it to mirror the sort of business it is for. A case of an awful name comes from a now old sweets store claimed and worked by a companion named Deborah. Her store was named "Debby Because." While it might have been easy to recall, would you be able to tell by the name that it was a treats store?

Most likely not. Names like Jane's Senior Service say somewhat more about the business and Jane's Senior Transportation Service would be far better. At the point when you include somewhat about the sort of service your business provides, it makes the business name easier to recall and it makes it a name that makes sense.

By focusing on all the tips referenced, you will give your senior transportation service an edge. That edge might be everything you require to launch into a successful business.

CHAPTER - 3

SENIOR TRANSPORTATION BUSINESS PLAN

To start a transportation business, you should choose which sort of business you plan to make. Options include: a taxi service, bicycle rental, limousine service, owner or administrator shipping, moving organization, specialized transportation service, livestock transportation, transporting boats, air transport, marine shipping, clinical transport or services for seniors. The kind of organization you use to establish should be resolved based, in addition to other things, on the need and rivalry in the zone you choose to work in. When you make sense of what you need to transport, you'll have to construct an arrangement to establish how you will offer these types of assistance.

The point of having business plan, showcasing ideas and strategies is so that you could characterize and coordinate the advertising activities that are expected to manufacture customer base, while also increasing income for your transportation business. It is something that encourages an association to look both internally and apparently, so as understand the effect of promoting decisions and the objective market. A showcasing strategy will make goals, whilst encouraging a business to extend.

Before completing your promoting strategies, you would need to decide your advertising financial plan. Starting another business, you may be needed to use more cash than a previously existing business would require, because of that reality that potential clients are not yet mindful of your services. At the point when your transportation business has gotten known, your advertising spending plan would then be able to tumble to an unimportant aspect of your income.

Critically, a business plan is a working archive that can change after some time. At the point when you are beginning in business, your business plan is a layout of what you need to do and how you will do it.

CHOOSING A SUITABLE LOCATION FOR YOUR SENIOR TRANSPORTATION BUSINESS

In an offer to start this business successfully, you should choose a suitable area for your business. For you to do this serenely, you need to make a careful assessment of costs. The ideal area should be one where costs are limited. You should have the option to take a gander at the advantages which every region has to offer as well as any administration help which may be accessible.

In this business, your decision of area should have easy access to all significant routes in your general vicinity and enough parking spots to safely store every one of your vehicles. A suitable area for your senior transportation business or a dispatch office for your senior transportation business should be easy to find, helpful for the taxis to be refueled and fixed. Halfway found sites are best in the event that you will serve your whole city.

- **Plan Out Your Finances**

Indeed, even with good thoughts and goals, lacking financing is a sand trap that will swallow up your splendid ideas. Finance in the senior transportation business is a major fixing especially on the off chance that you are hoping to start a huge scale senior transportation business.

Try not to get it confused, in fact with a telephone and a vehicle you can start a senior transportation business. What differentiates a small business and a huge scale business is advertising abilities and target markets. Nowadays getting funds for a business is not an easy task because nobody would need to vow his or her cash in a business that cannot ensure returns and profits. Examples of ways to get subsidizing may incorporate;

- Funds from Personal savings

- Getting loans from families and friends

- Investors

- Taking small business loans

- Getting microloans

- Attract a heavenly attendant investor

You should have cash so as to start your transportation business. To get an advance, you should show lenders and different investors a solid business plan.

This would incorporate what you hope to need to start your business, such as a vehicle, safety gear, and specialized devices. You will also need to insure your vehicle appropriately.

Showcasing ideas and Strategies

Individuals who have succeeded in business always have a solid establishment in showcasing. When anticipating the best method to sell your services, there are some different things you will also need to find out about advertising a senior transportation business.

Listen to Marketing Consultants

Undoubtedly, as someone hoping to start up small you may imagine that you have the stuff to advertise your image successfully. Possibly you do. According to understanding, there is no substitute for requiring the services of a certified advertising consultant. The best consultants possess a scope of skills, including the capacity to precisely convey your senior transportation business service' center competencies, worth and item points.

These things are the seemingly insignificant details which without the information can free you of precious opportunities in the commercial center. With the consistently changing senior transportation industry, the need has sought professional advertising to help convey an upper hand to your business.

Broadcast Advertising

Try not to see the decrease in the broadcast TV and radio industry as a chance to discount broadcast advertising totally. A ton of senior transportation services are leveraging broadcast media to perform specific aspects of their showcasing strategies. It is best for entrepreneurs to assess their intended interest group's listening or survey patterns and afterward tailor their media purchases to specific news sources as opposed to covering the topography with brand messaging.

Consider Media Monitoring

A great deal of promoting initiatives do loan themselves to simple measurement while others are additionally testing. For instance, standard mail can be assessed by counting the cost of inputs (for example an excellent mailing list, printing, postage, and so on.) and measuring the quantity of customer responses you get from the mission. Note that the trouble comes when you are tasked with evaluating market presence and brand impact.

Yet, nowadays, media checking has the capacity to give your senior transportation service a sense of market presence and different variables that are hard to evaluate. Whenever executed appropriately, media observing can enable your image to advance beyond negative messaging and apply more prominent impact over news cycles.

- **Winning Competitors in the Senior Transportation Business**

Successful business individuals have always been individuals who saw rivalry as a need to improve and make a stand. Rivalry is the thing that brings about ideas and inventiveness. Without rivalry, the transportation business would be exhausting and will need groundbreaking ideas and direction, and nobody will strive to satisfy the overall population.

Surely, ways to win your competitors in the senior transportation business is by noticing a void or an opening in the business and fill it serenely. A business does not necessarily need to be progressive so as to succeed. Instead of struggling to think of a spic and span thought, investigate the industry and see where there is a void to be filled. Note that your services might be similar in numerous aspects to that of the opposition aside from a couple of characterizing factors.

Secondly, to crush your competitors is to make a customer-driven culture by showing your drivers to show and display hospitality and benevolent personality. To understand costumer, need and listen to complains. You should make a bit of leeway and strive not to contend on prices.

Individuals may be glad to pay modest fares yet most individuals would contemplate their solace and happiness to the value they pay. Have it as a primary concern that a serious and swarmed industry indicates that customers request exists, and that the market is practical.

Strategies to boost your senior transportation business brand awareness and increasing corporate character brand awareness is tied in with winning customers and telling them what your identity is and what you offer. This is the reason you have to ensure you shout about your image and get your name before as numerous eyeballs as possible. It takes arranging and advancement to have the option to push your senior transportation business to a point where individuals can easily distinguish it and belittle you. Ideas for boosting your image awareness and making a corporate character may incorporate;

Using the web - With the approach of innovation and modernization, most homes and businesses on the planet are on the web, and cell phones normally have web access. It is suggested you advance your awareness by building up a website. Utilize a search motor enhancement organization or get familiar with the process all alone and sure that your website appears high in Web search results. Contact website owners in related industries to see on the off chance that you can put ads on their websites.

Making a social media presence - Social media sites such as Facebook and Twitter can be essential tools in creating brand awareness in the taxi business because they serve as forums where consumers discuss their lives, including their activities and items they like.

Family is not always accessible, the bus schedule may not be reliable, and numerous seniors need assistance to get from their home to the vehicle and afterward into the specialist's office. Have a go at asking a bus driver to do that. You can give some assistance, a solid, trustworthy ride and an inviting smile.

- **Insurance**

At the point when you start a transportation business, you should ensure that your vehicle meets the specialized models for the business you are running. Take as much time as necessary building up a business intend to ensure that you are really prepared.

You should investigate keep up legitimate insurance, both for your business itself, and for you drivers and vehicles, ensuring that all drivers and vehicles are appropriately insured as required by your jurisdiction. This could incorporate specialist's compensation insurance for your employees, or load insurance in the event that you ship. Once more, it depends on which sort of business you wish to establish.

- **Hardware**

Your business plan should show the hardware you will require, from the quantity of vehicles, to wheelchair lifts, down to printers and fax machines for your office activity. Check your state's requirements for gear. For instance, some states require a specific number of vehicles so as to establish a taxi fleet.

- **Employees**

In the event that you have to enlist employees, you should ensure that you enlist them as per the laws of your jurisdiction. For instance, you may need to obviously establish equivalent employing practices that are non-discriminatory. Ensure you understand the requirements in your state.

There are a ton of moving parts in establishing a transportation business, so do as much research as possible before setting out on your excursion.

CHAPTER - 4

CHOOSING A VEHICLE FOR SENIOR TRANSPORTATION BUSINESS

Starting A Van Transportation Business

Transportation business is one such business which has always been on the hit list of the entrepreneurs as it has an exceptionally impressive quantifiable profit on the off chance that you can oversee it well. Furthermore, the best part is you can start your transportation business with one single van or vehicle and afterward develop as you extend. So, let us see the basic requirements to start transportation business with just one van.

Vans are versatile vehicles and are regularly used in the transportation business. You can transport everything from passengers to payload using a van. Starting a van transportation business requires the vehicle overhead, business licensing and promoting to secure a spot in the neighborhood business condition. The biggest test is choosing the best specialty and narrowing down your objective market while building up a focused showcasing strategy.

- **Characterize the Niche**

The first step is to purchase or recruit the correct sort of van which is suitable for the kind of transport business you are getting in to. Principally for the transportation of the individuals, you have to see whether it will be for singular transport like cabs or it will be a pool system for which you will require a spaciously expanded van.

Since the web based business requires transportation services, you can also tie up with the internet business brands and give transportation service to their goods either inside the city or intercity and for this, you would require a major van which can oblige the items of the internet business So, the decision of the van would rely upon the kind of business you are getting into.

Working in a specific specialty is ideal for a van transportation business. You can always use the van for work outside of that specialty, however focusing on a specific market increases consumer certainty while lessening obscurity.

A couple of basic niches incorporate passenger transport, payload, dispatch service and clinical transport. You can truly limit things down if the market has sufficient work accessible for your specific specialty decision as well. For instance, a passenger service can focus specifically on inn and air terminal shuttles. Numerous hotels offer a shuttle service, yet getting your services in a busy city can transform into an all-day work, because hotels are frequently overbooked on shuttle services.

- **Niches for Van Transportation**

The passenger van transportation specialty can also work specifically for things like waterway shuttles in boating areas, senior resident transport services, or incapacitated transport with a wheelchair lift and special accommodations installed.

The clinical field has specific needs for hardware and supply transportation. Having an EMT affirmation can also prompt a worthwhile specialty transporting passengers with special ailments.

Dispatch services do not necessarily need a van, because they are frequently archive based however the model can still function admirably with an eco-friendly van model. In the payload transport space, the van will require expulsion of the passenger seating to focus on using an open space alongside secure strap points. Load can work in a more summed up business model, serving everything from home-moving to transporting significant items.

- **Orchestrate Finances**

The following and one of the most significant steps is orchestrating the finance to purchase or take a lease of the van. On the off chance that you effectively own a vehicle which is suitable as per your business type then you probably will not need to search for finance yet in the event that you have to purchase or recruit a van, you have to finance it. Besides the cost or lease of the van, do not invest cash in recruiting employees from the earliest starting point or orchestrating a legitimate office, start from your home or carport and drive all alone and deal with the business as well. You can take help from your family in the administration so that you can totally focus on the deliveries and the clients. This will diminish your cost of investment and increase the return.

- **Hardware and Licensing**

Purchase a van that truly fits your business model. A waterway shuttle service, for instance, may require a four-wheel-drive model to run soil roads in wet conditions. Ensure the van has abundant inside space, safe passenger seating and a secure freight territory to ensure significant items.

Subsequent to purchasing the van, you must license the business with your city and state. Functioning as an LLC or LLP on the off chance that you have an accomplice is ideal. The business license is simple, and it limits your personal risk which is especially significant in the transportation business. Acquire a business driver's license whenever required, as well. Numerous vans are fine on an ordinary license, yet huge vans may require a business grant to work.

There are four types of the distinctive grant which you have to acquire as indicated by the idea of your transport business. On the off chance that you are starting up a transport business with taxis or taxi, at that point there are contract carriages grant, for the transportation of the goods you need great carriages license, for the buses you would require stage carriages grant lastly for the two goods and individuals and passengers, you would require casual contact carriage grant. These permits are impermanent and for the time of 4-5 years after which you need to reestablish them. Besides these, you have to have your own license for driving the van or vehicle or on the off chance that you enlist a driver, he needs to have the same.

- **Business and Liability Insurance**

Obligation insurance is the following significant step. In a passenger van, your insurance must cover the driver alongside the passengers and the van itself. Freight vans will still require obligation insurance to secure the load and the driver. Try not to skimp on insurance, because it can save your business in case of a mishap.

Insuring the vehicle is by all account not the only thing you have to consider yet you have to also insure all the goods you are conveying starting with one spot then onto the next. The across the board insurance which is minimal costly can give genuine feelings of serenity to your customer and you at the same time. Since any harm to the vehicle or the goods inside it or to both because of awful street condition or mishap will be secured by the insurance so that you and your clients won't need to tolerate any loss.

- **Set up the Van for the Intended Use**

Lastly, set up your van to meet the expected use. A freight van requires secure points, straps and moving blankets to ensure the payload. A passenger van should always be perfect and definite. Set up a portable specifying pack to keep up a professional appearance. Include any specialty gear required for your specific business model.

- **Advertising and Operations**

After your van is prepared and the business is licensed, the time has come to hustle and construct your customers. Examination with nearby advertising on paper and computerized mediums.

Facebook and Instagram ads are always a decent starting point, because they are inexpensive. Manufacture a website and a functioning social media presence alongside your ads.

Entryway to-entryway sales are also profitable in the business to business space. In the event that you plan on collaborating with hotels or senior resident communities, reach them legitimately and pitch your services. Hit the asphalt and keep a point by point schedule to ensure you never twofold book. At the point when the schedule is consistently filled, you can consider adding extra vehicles and drivers to make a fleet.

- **Put your Van On the map**

When you are finished with all the above procedures, the last arrangement is to advance your business. Perhaps the best ways to advance your transportation business is to use the vinyl stickers with all the necessary data and contact details on the body of the van so that it catches the eyes of the individuals out and about. At that point you can also advance it on the web and proposal works the best regardless.

CHAPTER - 5

GROWING YOUR BUSINESS IN THE SENIOR TRANSPORTATION SERVICES

To be perfectly honest speaking, despite the fact that you are going to leave on a mind-boggling venture by establishing a senior transportation business, you cannot depend on just that to be successful. Sure, the quick aging of our populace points to an endless supply of expected customers yet you have to plan something for make your service stand out from all other transportation services accessible in your locale, district and state. Here are some tips that will help push your business in front of every other person.

1. The Extra Mile

You have most likely heard the expression, "going the additional mile" and I'm sure you realize it refers to customer service. Possibly, you have also experienced someone giving you their additional best service at one at once in your life. The way to being recognized as a decent business administrator comes from giving superior customer service. This most positively means going the "additional mile" or more for your clients. It can seem like a small gesture to some, however for huge numbers of your elderly clients, accomplishing something somewhat more will place you in a class all your own in their eyes.

2. Google Places

The web is an apparatus that makes everything a ton easier and, in this day, and age, we are always in a rush for data. Going to the computer for answers seems to be the pattern and so as to arrive at your computer savvy clients, you have to take an interest effectively on the web. A standout amongst other free ways of doing that is to have your business listed at Google Places. There are a couple of steps you have to follow to accomplish this, yet once you are there, your business will be easier to discover.

3. Do not Forgo the Logo

Some are fanatic of marking and picture design. There are some notorious ones that have meshed their way into our everyday consciousness after some time and have changed over from brand names to household terms. This is not to say you need your image to be as well known, however you will need it to be as essential. This can be accomplished by having a strong and easy to distinguish logo. You may even have the option to make your own logo for nothing on the web. Just search "free logo producer" and see what pops up. The free advertising it will restore your business will be immeasurable.

4. Blogging Your Service

By using any of several distinctive free online blog host programs such as blogger.com, you can dispatch a blog at no cost in practically no time. This is an incredible method to arrive at your customers rapidly and normally. With a blog you can share anything from up and coming service specials to details on yourself and your service. The extraordinary thing about blogging is that you can do it as little or as regularly as you wish. It gives your clients a taste of the 'genuine' you which builds trust. Actually, convincingly that by using a blog with your senior transportation business, the exposure will bring you much success.

5. Free Promotion and Advertising

There are various forms of free advertising that will profit your business. They incorporate online classified ads, business cards and posters. Notwithstanding, the best type of free advertising that will cost you nothing, business cards and posters are not free, is from the recommendations and referrals you will get from satisfied and glad customers. This goes back to tip number one where your customer service will win you steadfastness. Upbeat customers will talk up your senior transportation business and that is the thing that you need. Referrals are the best method to manufacture a business as you have been endorsed by someone who has just used your service.

CHAPTER - 6

FINDING NEW CUSTOMERS

The search for new customers drives most businesses. The present customers change their item and service providers routinely, so businesses need to endeavor to supplant lost customers and continue constructing their customer base.

Numerous small businesses struggle to discover new customers. Traditional approaches to discovering customers such as making 'cold pitches' and sales presentations can be troublesome and defying for small business owners who need sales and showcasing experience. Notwithstanding, there are an assortment of different ways that you can discover new customers, and with careful arranging you can improve your chances of success.

It is significant that your work to discover new customers does not stop you from conveying an elevated level of service to your existing customers. Satisfied customers who appreciate great customer service bring rehash business and contribute a huge level of your sales. They can also allude different buyers to your business.

Three Steps to Getting New Customers

- **Changing over contacts to leads**

In the present exceptionally serious markets, most small businesses strive to discover contacts and recognize new customer leads. The key is to discover individuals who fit your 'optimal lead profile'. Recollect that lone those contacts who need your products and match your optimal lead profile are probably going to become prospects for sales. Try not to waste your important time and cash on contacts who are probably not going to purchase from you.

Start by discovering contacts, and afterward use your optimal lead profile to transform those contacts into leads and new prospects. A lead does not turn into a customer until you have made the sale.

- **Discovering contacts**

Finding new contacts takes careful arranging. Make time to consider how you will discover and connect with contacts and research new customer opportunities. For instance, you may meet contacts at a career expo, through a business organization, or through a customer mailing list. Contacts could be any individual who visits, browses through your store, reads your advertising or are alluded to you by others.

- **Building up your optimal lead profile**

Leads are contacts who coordinate the profile of your objective customers. When you have met and engaged with another reach, you should decide if they have a requirement for your products and services. At the point when you have established that another contact fits your 'optimal lead profile', they become a lead.

Based on your statistical surveying, your optimal lead profile will characterize characteristics such as: geographic traits where the individuals or businesses liable to purchase from you are found demographics the age, sexual orientation, salary, occupation type, instruction level, social foundation, and household type (for example single, hitched, families) of individuals liable to purchase from your psychographics social factors such as lifestyle, interests and activities, opinions, self-picture and social gathering memberships.

CHAPTER - 7

RESOURCES

Senior Transportation resources can include the following.

1. Local Transportation organizations such as open buses and trains managed by neighborhood government.

2. Non-benefit Local Transportation Organizations which might be free or ease for qualifying riders. Ordinarily, they have small buses and vans that serve the network.

3. Dial-a-ride Organizations offering entryway to-entryway services which might be free or ease for qualifying riders. Ordinarily, they have small buses and vans that serve the network.

4. Paratransit Options, also known as access-a-ride which is transportation for the disabled and seniors offering entryway to-entryway services on a space accessible and reservation basis. This sort of transportation might be free or minimal effort for

qualifying riders. Normally, they have small buses and vans that serve the network.

5. Movement Organizations that offer sweeping care that regularly includes transportation for their members. Website: National Pace Association.

6. Senior Centers may have transportation to carry seniors to the middle and afterward take them home.

7. Network volunteers offering driving services through organizations such as the Village to Village organization or other beneficent organizations. Frequently there is a yearly expense to join the town association and afterward network volunteers offer types of assistance such as a ride to the specialist's office.

8. Bigger non-profits offering transportation such as United Way, American Red Cross, Volunteers of America and Easter Seals to give some examples.

9. Taxi Services which are expense for service revenue driven organizations

10. Clinical Transport companies such as rescue vehicle services for transportation required for clinical situations.

There are also private compensation homemaker-companions gave by organizations that will offer driving types of assistance, usually using the senior's own vehicle to drive them to appointments, errands and personal excursions.

CHAPTER - 8

HIRING EMPLOYEES

The recruiting process is a basic piece of maintaining any business. Regardless of whether you are a small business owner, a Human Resource (HR) director, or the Chief Executive Officer (CEO) of an enormous organization, you should enlist at some point in your career. Employing can pummel its own.

Regardless of how small your transportation business starts out; you may discover when you have to recruit help. Perhaps you start with subcontractors who take up the slack when you have a greater number of jobs than you can deal with. Possibly you recruit low maintenance driver who allows you to not drive on Fridays so you can complete office work or ensure some family time. However, in the event that you extend enough, you will wind up with employees, regardless of whether they are drivers or an accountant or a scheduler or whatever fringe duties should be done to prop your business up.

Choosing employees whether impermanent or lasting can be an arrangement creator, or breaker, for your developing organization. You need a solid group around you. Someone, regardless of whether yourself, a lasting staff part, or a transitory worker, will be expected to fill every one of the accompanying roles:

Office supervisor - Handles administrative, administrative, and office-supply duties like answering the phones, keeping the workplace perfect and clean, documenting, and perhaps in any event, organizing employees.

Sales staff - Someone whose activity it is to discover business and market your service.

Head of showcasing - In a small shop, this could be the salesperson's part as well dealing with advertising and advancement, and getting opportune exposure to the media.

Clerk - Tracks all business expenses, and may also plan government forms. On the off chance that you enlist a bookkeeper to do some of the more elevated level finance-related tasks, you might have the option to do the accounting yourself.

Note that the above list is about roles, not titles. There is considerable assortment in titles given to employees, yet whether you use casual titles or more proper ones, the tasks are the same. Also do not feel like you absolutely need to enlist a separate worker for every one of these duties. Almost certainly, you wind up satisfying all or most of these duties yourself.

Contacting candidates - When you have decided the kind of positions you have to fill, you should advertise these open positions. Try not to skimp on this step. Cast your net as generally as possible to gather the best employees.

Advertising - Consider putting an advertisement in your nearby and provincial newspapers. In the event that the activity you are filling is a more senior-level position in your transportation business, at that point also consider advertisements in bigger newspapers as well as exchange journals. These public ads, however, will be significantly more expensive, so plan on setting public ads just when the position warrants. Public searches will probably draw in candidates who should migrate so their salary expectations may also be higher so as to warrant a move.

Online newspaper advertising - Check with the advertising representative at your nearby paper to see if the newspaper offers an online choice. Most newspapers offer packages, including print just, online just, or the two types of advertising. In the event that the newspaper offers an online alternative, plan on setting an online as well as a print version of your advertisement.

Online places of work - Online business advertising on sites. Be that as it may, you truly are pulling in a public crowd whether you mean to make it clear in your advertisement where the activity is situated to get rid of remote who will probably not be moving 1,500 miles to take the activity.

Colleges and universities - Colleges and universities frequently have their own newspapers as well as websites on which you can post your employment opportunities. This is a brilliant source for finding capable candidates, especially for less-senior positions.

Verbal - Word of mouth is regularly significant in discovering key employees. Tell your vendors that you are searching for employees.

Meeting - As you start getting with prospective applicants, you will need to peruse their resumes and make a point system, perhaps from 1 to 10, offering 1s to inadequate candidates and 10s to top candidates. On the off chance that you composed an exact expected set of responsibilities, you should not have a huge number. Nor should you have a huge number of dream candidates are uncommon.

As you survey the resumes, use your rating system to choose which applicants to meet.

Meeting Strategies - Plan on meeting five to ten applicants for more senior positions, less for less senior openings. At the point when a candidate arrives for a meeting, have them complete an application structure. You will need to ask all candidates the same series of questions, ensuring a reasonable process. Contact your industry's exchange association, which may have the option to offer questions that would be pertinent to your specific transportation business.

Take notes during interviews so you can survey them later and winnow your candidates to two finalists. Ask these two back for a second meeting. Take notes so you can access responses of the two candidates after the interviews and make a last selection.

After the second meeting, you should compose an offer letter to the triumphant competitor, spreading out your proposal, complete with pay structure and benefits. When you and the candidate have signed the letter, you should tell the other finalist that the position is filled. Hold up until the triumphant candidate has officially acknowledged before telling the losing applicant the terrible news. Too often, the triumphant up-and-comer will decrease the offer, and you will need to have the option to go to your second applicant.

Pay - There are numerous variables to consider while paying your staff. For instance, in more metropolitan areas of the nation, pay tends to be higher. Compensation is also based on the representative's understanding and measure of responsibility.

Preparing - In the event that you are recruiting drivers, you will probably be employing someone who has at any rate experienced truck driving school or has a business license for the specific sort of driving required for your business. The bigger shipping companies have their own schools.

Past that, you still need to consider preparing your employees, regardless of whether they are freshman drivers just out of school or bookkeepers or schedulers. These employees need to stay informed concerning the latest trends in the transportation industry and ability to use the most modern tools to carry out their responsibilities adequately and productively.

Be a decent boss and set aside the effort to satisfactorily prepare your recently recruited employees, and assume the best about them for raising rapidly to an acceptable level. At the point when they show up for their first day of work, show them how you like things done, where the things are that they have to play out the activity they were recruited to do, and the basics of your activity.

There is simply nothing more frustrating for another representative than being left to flop. Plan on furnishing every representative with an itemized set of working responsibilities, outlining his or her responsibilities. Furthermore, acquaint new employees with everybody in the business or organization so they meet the new team of individuals they will be working with.

CHAPTER - 9

SOME TIPS FOR SENIOR TRANSPORTATION BUSINESS

TRANSPORTATION OPTIONS FOR SENIORS WHO DO NOT DRIVE

As seniors retire from driving and start investigating elective transportation options, they may locate that reasonable and proper options are restricted or inaccessible. This has immediate and aberrant consequences for seniors, their caregivers, and society. The powerlessness to get all over town can prompt isolation, restricted access to necessary clinical supports and services, and decreased network interest. Thus, government can wind up attempting to fix the problems made by an absence of transportation with costly interventions, as the total impact of these consequences challenge the capacity of seniors to develop old in the communities, they call home.

So, what are the current transportation alternatives that are offered to seniors? We can start by taking a gander at the obvious options such as strolling, and work through to transit, taxis, HandyDART, friends and family and network volunteers. Every choice will offer some seniors some utility as an option in contrast to driving. Be that as it may, no alternative can offer all seniors a down to earth substitution for all their transportation needs.

Aside from driving themselves, for seniors living autonomously, dependence on friends and relatives is the following most basic type of transportation. As seniors age, they are increasingly bound to go as passengers. While 38% of non-driving seniors aged 65 to 74 are a passenger in a vehicle as their essential type of transportation, this increases to almost 60% for seniors more than 85 years higher than some other type of transportation. Indeed, even seniors who can use public transportation may depend on friends or relatives to get around probably some of the time.

To understand the challenges of using public transportation for seniors with intellectual, portability or other health challenges, the entirety of the components associated with finishing a public transportation venture must be considered.

A run of the mill excursion using public transportation requires:

Knowing where your nearby bus stop is found and having the option to stroll to it and stand and hang tight for as long as 15 minutes.

Knowing the nearest bus stop to your destination and having the option to stroll from that stop to your last destination.

Realizing which bus or buses to catch to get to your destination.

Comprehending what time your bus(es) run. Many buses have regular service during rush hour however others are sometimes just every 30 or an hour during non-top hours, and there are frequently various schedules for quite a long time and holidays.

Realizing how long it will take to get to your destination once you are on the bus.

Knowing how much the bus toll will be and having the specific change, or heading off to a close by store or candy machine to purchase bus tickets and additionally a pass.

Presently envision a 87-year-old who has not taken a bus in 70 years. They have surrendered their driver's license because their macular degeneration has delivered them legitimately visually impaired, and they struggle currently to use the PC and cannot dependably peruse print material. They are still intellectually fit and use a walker for balance yet could surely walk three blocks to a bus stop. On the off chance that the climate is acceptable and they are feeling great on that specific day they could take the bus.

Actually, numerous seniors would be safer and more agreeable, in the event that they had easy access to exchange personal transportation. So, what are the options?

The following, is the breakdown of transportation options for seniors who do not drive, including the pros and cons of every alternative.

- **Public Transportation Routes**

Public transportation is a generally inexpensive approach to get around most cities and towns. Two normal forms of mass public transit you may exploit incorporate bus routes and metro or subway routes. The pros of public transportation incorporate low fares, the capacity to access nearby programs for assistance paying those fares and the dependability of routes. Disadvantages incorporate a need to live approach city routes, the way that you may need to stroll to stations or stops and an absence of accessibility.

Not all mass transit options are promptly accessible for individuals who depend on wheelchairs or walkers. To see whether buses in your city offer wheelchair ramps or lifts, visit your regional's administration website or call nearby transit authority offices. Also ask for data about toll discount programs. Numerous metro areas offer diminished fares for senior citizens, and you may be qualified for admission assistance in the event that you are on a fixed salary.

The National Aging and Disability Transportation Center publishes instructive resources for seniors and communities. One pamphlet helps cities make bus stops safe and accessible, however the data in the download may also assist seniors with bettering assess services to ensure they are safe to use.

In the event that you are situated in a zone served by open transportation, at that point you are in luck! Public trains, subways, buses, and other transport can be an extraordinary decision for seniors, especially on the off chance that they are still moderately portable. Be that as it may, if not it goes another route round.

- **Taxi Services**

Taxi services are a decent alternative for seniors who live in suburban or rustic areas just outside of the city. These services do not depend on topography as intensely as mass transit solutions do, and you can have the service get you at your home. Different benefits of taxi services incorporate as-required scheduling and one-on-one assistance which can be useful in the event that you are conveying items or have a walker or stick. The biggest disadvantage of taxi services is the cost when contrasted with mass transit.

Find customary taxi services in your general vicinity by starting with the telephone directory or a Google search on the web. Browsing listings online lets you read reviews, causing it almost certain you to associate with a quality organization and get some answers concerning accessibility options. You can also download various taxi apps in the event that you have a smartphone. Apps such as Easy Taxi let you flag down a taxi from your cell phone.

In some areas, you can save cash by using a group service such as Uber, however most experts suggest drawing nearer Uber and similar models with alert. On the off chance that you are new to swarm services, consider asking for assistance the first barely any times you use the application, and in the event that you are ever awkward with the situation when your Uber driver does show up, do not hesitate to adjust your perspective.

- **Volunteer Driving Programs**

Organizations such as public venues, churches, and non-profits regularly run volunteer driving programs. Individuals volunteer to drive others to and from clinical appointments or on errands. The advantage of such programs is that the association has usually given in any event basic reviewing of volunteers, so you can ride with less risk and with no cost to you. The disadvantage is that volunteer time is usually restricted, so you need to schedule rides well ahead of time and you may not always have a ride when you need it.

Social programs, non-profits, religious organizations, and other volunteer organizations regularly accumulate around cities, suburban communities, and senior living hotspots to offer free and minimal effort transportation for seniors.

For data about volunteer driving programs in your general vicinity, contact public venues and churches. In the event that you have accessibility issues, ensure you specify those in advance. Some organizations permit volunteers to drive individuals in their own cars while others have accessible vans for transportation purposes.

- **Clinical Facility Transportation**

Some clinical facilities offer restricted transportation options for patients who cannot get to the clinics or hospitals. While most stand-alone physician offices cannot bear to run such programs, if your doctor is essential for a bigger gathering or works in a hospital complex, they may offer minimal effort or free clinical van transportation for appointments.

On the off chance that your supplier does not offer transportation, businesses and network organizations frequently specialize in clinical transport or paratransit services. Benefits of professional clinical transport incorporate wheelchair accessible vehicles and drivers and assistants who may be prepared to deal with minor clinical issues. Some clinical transport services are also secured under state Medicaid plans, especially in the event that you need to go outside of your geographic zone for specialty, non-crisis clinical care.

Did you realize that Medicaid provides non-crisis transportation to and from clinical services? To fit the bill for NEMT services, seniors must:

- Be qualified for Medicaid;

- Not have a legitimate driver's license;

- Not have a working vehicle accessible in the household;

- Be unfit to travel or sit tight for services alone; or

- Have a physical, psychological, mental, or formative constraint

Of course, this covers just transportation to and from clinical appointments.

- **Door through Door Private Transportation**

In numerous metropolitans, suburban, and even some rustic communities, taxi services and private transportation agencies are outfitted to seniors and offer on-request, entryway to-entryway, and even entryway through-entryway transportation. Senior-accommodating services offer assistance with walkers, wheelchairs, and bags (counting basic food item bags), for a mileage and time sensitive expense.

- **Discovering Community and Paratransit Services**

On the off chance that the elders throughout your life require wheelchairs or have different disabilities, research the accessibility of ADA para-transit services in your general vicinity. These services might be worked both secretly or openly, and commonly supplement fixed bus and rail routes in your general vicinity.

The overall principle for paratransit services states that vans and microbuses must be furnished with ADA facilities, and must run inside 3/4 mile of existing bus or train stations, on the same schedules, and for close to 2x the cost of standard fares.

For some seniors, the biggest obstacle to accessible transportation is simply getting some answers concerning the service. Instead of spending hours on the telephone finding transportation options, start with Eldercare.gov. Using the site's locale assistance finder, you can specify your postal district or city and search for resources and services identified with transportation. Eldercare.gov also provides a free booklet you can download itemizing extra options for transportation as a senior who does not drive.

- **Supplemental Transportation Programs for Seniors (STPs)**

In numerous metropolitan and metro areas, organizations work STPs: minimal effort, network based, and autonomously subsidized transportation services for seniors. Frequently staffed by volunteers, these programs are financed through an assortment of grants and donations, empowering them to offer profoundly responsive, moderately practical on-request transportation.

VARIOUS TRANSPORTATION BUSINESSES AVAILABLE

In start your own transportation service, the staff of business visionary media explains how you can dispatch a beneficial transportation service, regardless of whether you need to start a long stretch activity or an around service. This section will quickly discuss the ways you can begin in the transportation industry.

The accompanying represents a significant number of the possible types of transportation businesses you could choose to start. Everything depends on what your personal interest is and what skills you need to utilize in your business.

- **Taxi service**

Despite its underlying controversy and claims of out of line rivalry, Uber has staked its case across the world actually, in 400 cities and 65 countries. Uber's fascination as a small-business open door is that you are a self-employed entity and on your own schedule. To sign up as a driver, start by setting off to Uber's website, and snap on the "Become a Driver" button. A short questionnaire initiates the process.

As a driver, you use your own vehicle, so startup costs are moderately low. Uber handles all the financial aspects of the ride. Installment to the driver is consistently. As self-employed entities, drivers take on overhead costs (gas, support, insurance, and so forth.) themselves.

- **Bike rental**

Leasing bicycles is a flourishing business in specific areas. The two key environments where leasing bikes is a characteristic are in recreational tourism areas and cities. In tourism areas, you may hope to set up almost an enormous inn or resort where broadened vacations stays make prepared customers. In this sort of business, you will require a storefront as well as a space to store all your rental bikes.

Another possibility for bike rentals is a bike sharing methodology like Hub way. Bike stands around the city permit riders to lease a bike in one spot, ride to their area, and drop the bike at a stand close to their destination. Hubway offers yearly or month to month membership or day by day passes. Perhaps your town is prepared for a small-scale version of this business.

- **Limousine service**

You could give limo service to celebrities or to customary individuals.

At whatever point anybody is entrusting you to drive them, a spotless notoriety is significant. In any case, on account of the personal limo service, normally you will be driving a gathering of individuals who are not focusing on where you are going or how you are driving however are appreciating the ride. The driver needs to be supremely trustworthy, and the vehicle needs to be safe and well - kept up.

You can work the limo yourself, and your armada of one limousine will be moderately easy to keep up. You can give all the service yourself, from scheduling to driving. In the event that you need to grow, just include vehicles and drivers, and continue extending your showcasing to keep business streaming.

- **Owner or Operator shipping**

The basic organization of the shipping business is to offered on and satisfy contracts. As indicated by the SBA, there are two basic forms of working, with the key contrast being the means by which you get drivers to satisfy those contracts (or accounts on the off chance that your agreement to do the entirety of the shipping for a business):

Subcontract drivers - Drivers, in this case, are self-employed entities who probably own their own gear. You will spend your experience on two key coordination pieces getting the contracts and accounts with the manufacturers who need goods transported and afterward discovering drivers who can satisfy those contracts on schedule. The favorable position is lower costs self-employed entities not just usually have their own vehicles that they keep up themselves however they insure them and themselves as well.

Insurance is a tremendous cost factor in the transportation business, so unmistakably this is a savings. In any case, you will also be paying them a higher charge than if you were paying your own drivers, which cuts into profits. The genuine exchange here may be in less headaches as long as you feel sure of the drivers you enlist.

Secretly "possessed" drivers - In this scenario, you own the trucks and the drivers work for you. You have all out control and hold all benefit and you pay the entirety of the expenses of employees and gear, which means higher startup as well as higher working costs. While your drivers will be at your service for the accounts and contracts you hold, the pressure is on to have no vacation because you are paying for those drivers and those vehicles whether you are using them or not.

In the event that organizing and scheduling is a greater amount of your strong suit, you may find that setting up your business using contracted drivers is the best approach. Or then again perhaps a blend of both a sensible number of drivers and size of your claimed armada with a stable of agreement drivers to approach when you get a bigger number of contracts than you can deal with.

- **Moving van business**

Starting a small moving business is generally easy which also means you have to remember that you will probably be rivaling undergrads who use a leased box truck. Your ace card will be that you will set up and lead your business professionally, perhaps offering add-on services such as space for impermanent, in the middle of moves storage.

Startup costs remember purchasing at least one trucks for a scope of sizes that will oblige the sort of moving you intend to do. Also, of course, you will require a spot to stop them.

You will require in any event one worker you cannot lift that sofa alone. Furthermore, you should prepare that representative for pressing, moving procedures, customer interactions, how to act properly in a customer's home, and so forth., so your professional notoriety is not damaged.

- **Specialty transportation**

Specializing in a specific sort of unusual transportation incredibly huge items such as plane parts, or secluded houses, or refrigerated perishables, blood, or human organs can give a healthy pay. You will probably have less clients yet can charge higher fees for the expertise you have or gain from specializing.

Contingent upon where you are found will direct whether you can do this business yourself or need employees.

- **Livestock transportation**

Despite the fact that you need not bother with a specific licenses for transporting personal horses for customers unless you get into business size vehicles that hold numerous animals, you will require equine or cow-like understanding for possible clients to trust your capacity to transport their animals, and you have to acclimate yourself with the livestock transport regulations for crossing state lines.

Despite the fact that the livestock owner will be responsible for having their creature prepared for transport to its last destination, you will need to know the livestock regulations of any state you will enter. Most states have at any rate least requirements of certain infectious tests (counting a health test) or potentially vaccinations for entering their state.

Try not to surrender it to horse or steers owners to know these regulations; while they might be the one arranging and paying the veterinarian who will do these tests, you will need to be educated to advise them. It is to your advantage to ensure they have the correct desk work for you to show at the last destination or anyplace en route that is necessary.

To ensure the excursion goes smoothly for the creature, you should be proficient about livestock or recruit someone to do the real transport who is learned. Remember that on the off chance that you are transporting any distance and need to expedite, you should get the creature on and off the trailer several times. What is more, in addition to the fact that you need to realize how to manage things out and about tricks to get the horse to drink while voyaging and help stay away from colic, how to treat or swathe an injury if necessary you also need to know the basics behind driving carefully while towing a live creature. Getting a veterinary professional license or carrying an ensured vet tech with you may be useful and give you an edge for getting customers and verbal praise.

- **Boats**

Transporting boats is another specialty business that can be rewarding and interesting on the off chance that you are in a sea zone. Remember that this will be a seasonal business and very busy during the pre and post sailing season since everybody will need their vessel in the water or removed from the water in the same general time period.

You should choose what sort of boats you need to transport. A speedboat for the lake has a totally different trailer prerequisite than a huge sailboat with a mast and a fall. In spite of the fact that speedboat transport would probably be a higher-volume business, it is also something many pontoon owners can do themselves. Yet, on the off chance that you keep your prices reasonable and get known for taking additional great care of the boats you transport, you may discover individuals recruiting you to deal with this for them at any rate. Speedboat owners are probably going to have space in their yard to store them, yet on the off chance that you can give secured storage, you can have an additional worth part to your business. You can also include the service of shrink-wrapping the vessel before storage.

The startup subsidizing for vessel transport is modest however perhaps surprisingly higher than you may might suspect, especially given the cost of pickup trucks. You will require a properly sized truck and perhaps a few distinctive sized trailers. Also significant is risk insurance to cover the boats you transport and the possibilities of things that can happen when you pull things. That storage choice is a decent expansion aspect to the pontoon pulling business.

- **Air transport**

Transport via air, regardless of whether plane or helicopter, involves significant startup costs for gear, licensing (for yourself as well as employees), and insurance. Small plane transport can be of goods or individuals like hunters or skiers went too far off an area, conveying goods or mail to islands, or in any event, transporting cargo universally.

You would need to get your ducks straight using an office that has great freight taking care of and inspection hardware (especially for farming products and different items profoundly directed when they move around the nation) and customs in the event that you intend to do any worldwide shipping since moving products via air is about speed.

- **Marine shipping**

Transport by vessel is an enormous business. It is also an immense business to start. Marine shipping is regularly done by tankers stacked with containers that get lifted off the trailer of an 18-wheeler and stacked on the pontoon, commonly entails worldwide import or fare business, and requires information on customs regulations when all is said in done and for specific merchandise. On the off chance that you are a specialist scheduler and facilitator, perhaps this is the business for you. Be that as it may, similar to air transport, be ready for a great deal of research, arranging, and requirement for significant startup resources.

- **Clinical transport**

Clinical transport is a significant business in the transportation field. There are several ways to focus this business. Some require close to a standard vehicle, driver's license, and a solid driving record. You could focus on transporting seniors to clinical appointments locally, or, on the off chance that you live in a territory that is some distance from a city, you could focus on driving individuals' significant distances to specialist appointments at elite hospitals.

On the off chance that you have an EMT license, other clinical credentials, or are eager to get them, you could start a business that contracts with hospitals to drive conceded patients to other clinical facilities for specialized treatment; this would also require some specialty hardware like oxygen conveyance and perhaps a vehicle that can transport a patient in a wheelchair.

- **Senior services**

America is aging at a fast movement. As more established citizens relinquish their driver's licenses, there is open door for driving seniors to places they can no longer take themselves. Past clinical appointments, you could drive seniors to the market or to outings at the shopping center. On the off chance that you are in a region where seniors will in general be low-salary, you could consider setting up as a charitable and getting award support to help seniors in your area be more versatile. Award funders, corporate sponsors, and the central government are frequently hoping to use their funds for human service programs going to the guide of the weakest citizens.

CHAPTER - 10

FREQUENTLY ASKED QUESTIONS ON STARTING A SENIOR TRANSPORTATION BUSINESS

Starting a senior transportation business is much easier that starting most different businesses because it is a service business that does not need a store or stock. The interest is developing fast for senior transport drivers because of the enormous number of aging Americans who cannot drive anymore and need a ride to clinical appointments, shopping and social events. In the event that you have just found out about this business opportunity, you most likely have a couple of questions before you are prepared to begin.

Here are some of the most ordinarily asked questions:

1. What does a senior transportation business do?

One out of five seniors more than 65 does not drive, and needs to get to and from clinical appointments, such as a visit to their primary care physician or physical therapist. Also, just like the rest of us, non-driving seniors need to go out to shop, gotten things done, visit friends and go to social events. The fast-developing interest for private senior transportation services has made an enormous open door for those who can give rides to seniors and others who can't drive.

2. What hours do you need to work?

Because you are an autonomous service supplier, you have a considerable amount of power over your work routine. Most of your driving jobs will be during typical working hours (9 am to 5 pm) yet there can be occasional night work, contingent upon your customer's transportation needs. In the event that you want to work just low maintenance say 20 hours out of every week, you can regularly orchestrate that with your customers.

3.Who can use the Elderly Transportation Program?

The Elderly Transportation Program is given through MTM and is to some residents of 60 years old enough and more established who do not approach any means of transportation.

4. What amount do I get paid for driving seniors to and from their clinical appointments.

A senior transportation business commonly charges somewhere in the range of $30 and $60 60 minutes. Rates are higher in bigger cities and lower in smaller towns, where the cost of living is lower. In the event that you work an 8-hour day, it is possible to make a pay somewhere in the range of $60,000 and $120,000 per year.

5. Do I need special insurance?

Yes, you should have obligation insurance and accident protection inclusion for business use of your vehicle. The most effective method to start a beneficial senior transportation business, there are some public insurance representative who specialize in senior transportation business insurance, who can give you the inclusion you need at a serious cost.

6. Would i be able to get rides to a pharmacy?

You may not get an excursion specifically to go to a pharmacy, anyway you may have a ride there as a major aspect of your outing to or from another service.

7. What are the most well-known senior transportation services?

Each customer is unique, however most of your work will be taking seniors to their clinical appointments, such as specialist's visits, or customary visits to dialysis or physical treatment. As your customers become more acquainted with you, they will also ask you to drive them on personal trips, such as shopping for food, errands and to social events.

8. Where would i be able to get a ride to when using the Elderly Transportation Program?

The Elderly Transportation Program provides transportation to and from clinical appointments, grown-up day care, feast sites, dialysis or malignant growth treatment and the Insight Program.

9. Is a senior transportation business expensive to start?

Not under any condition in the event that you as of now have a solid vehicle. Aside from a vehicle, you will require a smartphone to stay in contact with your customers and schedule your rides.

At the point when you start out, you will require business cards and flyers or brochures to pass out to expected customers and health care providers who allude customers to you. By using reasonable online printers like Vistaprint.com and uprinting.com, you can complete your printing at a discount and likely spend less.

10. What amount notice is expected to drop transportation?

Please drop transportation as soon as you learn you will not need it.

11. Imagine a scenario where I have never done this.

In the event that you are a careful, safe driver, and you appreciate helping individuals, you have the most significant two skills you need. The driving trips are a lot of like what you as of now do each week with one significant contrast now you get paid for driving! A senior transportation service is about individuals, so the capacity to be a companion, a decent listener and have a bright demeanor and a can-do disposition is significant as well.

12. Would i be able to call with less than two business days' notification?

Transportation requests can be made every minute of every day for dire clinical appointments.

13. How would I find new customers without spending a great deal of cash?

The best strategy is verbal, because when you work admirably for a senior customer, they will tell their friends. Another almost free strategy is to leave a simple flyer or pamphlet at your neighborhood senior focus and nearby specialist's office and clinics. That can acquire numerous new customers as well.

14. Does starting a senior transportation business require specialized preparing?

Because you will give non-crisis clinical transportation (N.E.M.T.), you need not bother with clinical preparing, albeit almost all drivers take the reasonable CPR and First Aid classes offered at nearby Red Cross centers.

15. I am a Medicaid Member; would i be able to still use the Elderly Transportation Program?

Yes, on the off chance that you meet the age necessity and do not approach any means of transportation, you may use the Elderly Transportation Program for rides to feast sites and the Insight Program.

16. Do I need a specialized vehicle, similar to a wheelchair van?

No, because for each customer that is wheelchair bound, there are a lot more who are wandering (ready to walk). What is more, numerous who are in wheelchairs can be assisted getting in and out of a vehicle, and the wheelchair can be stored in the storage compartment in transit.

The best vehicles for transporting seniors are bigger sedans, SUVs and Mini-vans. It is significant for senior customers to have the option to get in and out of a vehicle easily, and bigger vehicles will in general be better for that.

17. Is there actually a great deal of work for a neighborhood senior transportation service?

There are more than 48-million seniors in the U.S and more than 5-million in Canada. That number is developing quickly, as 10,000 individuals turn 65 consistently! One of every five seniors' does not drive and needs transportation to clinical appointments, errands and social events.

18. Do I need to sign anything when I get my ride?

Yes, you are needed to sign the driver's log or electronic gadget upon get of the transport.

19. Would i be able to get mileage reimbursement?

No, there is no mileage reimbursement choice for the Elderly Transportation Program.

20. What sort of transportation will I get?

Types of transportation accessible:

a. Public Bus,

i. in the event that you live inside ½ mile of a bus stop,

ii. also, your healthcare office is inside ½ mile of a bus stop,

iii. also, you can walk ½ mile and

iv. you understand normal signs and bearing so as to get transportation from the accompanying modes of transport, your healthcare supplier must affirm your requirement for that degree of transport:

b. Vehicle/Minivan in the event that you cannot go for the bus or stroll

c. Wheelchair Van in the event that you:

i. are limited to a wheelchair or ADA consistent scooter

ii. require a lift prepared or move up wheelchair van

iii. need help of a prepared professional

CONCLUSION

Senior citizens need to get around and get things done just like every other person, regardless of whether it be an outing to the market, cleaners or specialist's office. It tends to be hard for some more established individuals to do the things they need and need to complete, frequently because of vision, hearing or portability problems. For these seniors, a transportation service custom-made to their needs can come in convenient and assist them with carrying on with a free life.

Starting up an elderly transportation business is opportune. With the quick rate where Baby Boomers are turning out to be seniors, there is a genuine interest for any sort of business that provides a service to seniors. This means there is a requirement for your business and will keep on being an interest for quite a long time into what is to come.